HOW TO BE A BEAUTIFUL

Bride

HOW TO BE A BEAUTIFUL

Bride

The Ultimate Guide on Creating Your Polished Wedding Image

AMIE WITKOWSKI

TATE PUBLISHING & *Enterprises*

Published by Tate Publishing & Enterprises, LLC
127 E. Trade Center Terrace | Mustang, Oklahoma 73064 USA
1.888.361.9473 | www.tatepublishing.com

Tate Publishing is committed to excellence in the publishing industry. The company reflects the philosophy established by the founders, based on Psalm 68:11,
"The Lord gave the word and great was the company of those who published it."

Published in the United States of America

ISBN: 978-1-60799-960-7
Reference / Weddings
09.09.22

Dedication

To my husband, Bret, the love of my life,
thank you for making my **DREAM** come true.
Thank you for inspiring me and believing in me.

To our daughters, Elizabeth and Emily,
a daily reminder that **DREAMS** do come true. Thank
you for your constant love and your laughter.

To my parents, Jim and Caryl Meister,
for encouraging me to always follow my **DREAMS**.

To God, who allows me to live my **DREAM**
Photographing Weddings!

Table of Contents

Foreward

Years ago I learned to never take advice from anyone with whom you'd not like to change places. If you wouldn't want what she has, or be as she is, don't listen to her opinion on what you should do, say, or be. In other words, you probably wouldn't take financial and business pointers from someone on government assistance.

For eleven years I have watched Amie Witkowski and have been amazed at her congruity: what she says, she does and is. She is the complete package, as her immaculate grooming, her cheerful nature, and her willingness to learn and be amazed work together to make so many who meet her and say, "Wow! I'd like to be like that!" The demonstration of Amie's success as a photographer and example of how she works with people was given to my entire family as she photographed my daughter's wedding, and years later, as she documented my husband's retirement with beautiful family pictures. To a person, we agreed that listening to Amie's suggestions and having her as our photographer ensured extra quality and satisfaction with the finished product.

As you are planning this very important day in your life, keep in mind that being teachable and willing to take advice from a real professional will pay off for you in so many ways. Your memories and your pictures will testify to the accuracy and suitability of the wonderful advice contained within the following pages. Congratulations on taking advice from a professional eager to mentor you!

—*Lou Pagel*
Mrs. Southwest Michigan 2001

Introduction

In 1966, my father, Jim Meister, established Meister Photography. At the age of fourteen, I became his assistant, and together we have photographed over five hundred weddings. I am proud to say I am a second generation photographer. It has been a privilege working along the side of my father as well as my mother, Caryl Meister, who was our business manager. Together they have taught me values and business skills that will last a lifetime. In 2006, my husband Bret and I purchased the Studio and added our last name, Witkowski to reflect the change.

I have seen many brides come across my lens. It is with this experience and knowledge that I want to share with you all the hints, tips, and secrets that I have learned over the years.

This book will help you create your polished image. It's the day you've dreamed of and planned for, next to saying yes, choosing your elegant image maybe your most inspired decision. This book will help you create your ultimate wedding image.

SLEEK AND *Sophisticated*

A GUIDE TO CHOOSING YOUR PERFECT WEDDING GOWN AND ACCESSORIES

Silk, tulle, satin, and chiffon… Nothing could be more important than choosing the perfect gown. The best wedding gown flatters a bride's features, emphasizing a good figure or creating the illusion of a better shape. Every bride wants to look beautiful on her wedding day, and this guide will help you achieve just that. There is a wedding gown style to flatter every figure. A wedding gown should celebrate the feminine form, achieving the look of sophisticated, grand, classic, innocent, contemporary, or romantic. Finding the perfect wedding gown, veil, and accessories is an exciting time for a bride, so enjoy the journey!

BRIDAL GOWN STYLES

There are six different body types that dress designers keep in mind when creating the perfect gown; hourglass, round, inverted, pear, straight, and diamond. An hourglass figure has small bone structure, a defined waist, curved hips, and a larger bustline. A woman with a round-shaped figure has a generous bust, a fuller back, generous middle, narrow hips, and slender legs. An inverted figure, is that of an inverted triangle with broad shoulders, a medium bust, an average waist, narrow hips, and shapely, long legs. A pear shaped body has a slender neck, narrow shoulders, small bust, a shapely waist, generous lower hips and fuller thighs. The straight body type is distinguished by an upper and lower torso, that are equal in width, an average bust, an undefined waist, a flat bottom, and slender legs. And lastly, a diamond shape body has narrow shoulders, a small bust, broad hips, and generous thighs. By knowing what body type you are, it will simplify your decision on choosing the perfect wedding gown.

BRIDAL GOWN STYLES

A-line: Starts close to the body at the top, then flares gently away (no pleats or gathers) like the letter "A" in its name.

Empire: The bodice ends just below the bustline and has a slim skirt flowing out beneath it.

Mermaid: This ultra-slim-fitting dress follows your every curve and then finishes with a flourish, slightly belled out, at the hem like a mermaid's tail.

Princess: The dress is fitted through the waist and then flares gently out. It has no waistline; instead, the side seams shape it.

Sheath: This slinky style follows your bodyline and has a fitted waistline and narrow skirt.

Basque: This is a tight, elongated bodice that comes to a "V" in the front.

Dropped: The waistline of the dress falls below your actual waist.

Natural: The bodice and skirt of the dress are joined right at your waist.

GOWN LENGTHS

Ballerina: Falls to or slightly below the center of the calf.

Floor: Rests about an inch from the floor. Most traditional length.

Knee: Rests slightly above the knee. Non-traditional length.

Mini: Rests slightly above the knee. Often chosen by second-time brides or brides that may be in a destination wedding.

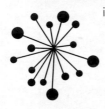

Cathedral: Longer than one yard. Usually reserved for the most formal weddings.

Chapel: Formal, extends about one yard.

Court: Separate piece of fabric that falls from the shoulders.

Detachable: Normally attached at back of your waist, but may attach to your shoulders or wrap around your waist.

Sweep: Just brushes the floor.

Watteau: Cascades from the shoulders.

NECKLINES

Band: The collar of this neckline encircles your neck. It has a look similar to that of a mock turtleneck.

Bateau: This is a high neckline that extends to the shoulders.

Halter: This sleeveless design encircles the neck, leaving your shoulders and back bare.

AMIE WITKOWSKI

Jewel:	A rounded neckline that slightly scoops to follow your collarbone, giving your pearl or jeweled necklace the showcase it deserves.
Crew:	Similar to the Jewel, but it falls higher on the neck.
Off-the-Shoulder:	A low neckline that extends around the upper part of the arms and bares the shoulders.
Portrait:	An off-the-shoulder neckline that owes its name to the way it frames the face. It often has a folded neckline that stands away from the body.
Scoop:	This is a low neckline, which can be cut deep in the front, back, or both.
Sweetheart:	This charming style looks like it sounds … a modest, heart-shaped finish to the front accentuating the bustline.
Tip of the Shoulder:	A just-barely-off-the-shoulder neckline.
V-neck:	Just like it sounds, a "V" in front or in back.

SLEEVES

Cup: These barely-there sleeves cover just your shoulders.

Fitted: The sleeves stay close to your arms. You can find them in various lengths.

Illusion: Sleeves made of a very fine net, nearly transparent.

T-shirt: These sleeves are straight and fall halfway between your shoulder and elbow.

Three-Quarter: These sleeves break between your wrist and elbow.

Juliet: Long, fitted sleeves with short puffs at your shoulders.

Wedding Point: V-shaped extension of a long, fitted sleeve that comes to a point over your wrist.

HEADPIECES

Floral Wreath: Worn over the forehead or nestled in your hair.

Juliet Cap: Fits tightly to the crown of your head and it may be made entirely of pearls or jewels.

Mantilla: Lace veil worn over your face.

Profile:	Decorative comb worn on one side of your head, silhouetting your face.
Tiara:	A crown that rests on top of your head.

VEILS

Ballet or Waltz:	Comes to just an inch above the floor.
Bird Cage:	Stiff. Covers the face, falls just below your chin.
Blusher:	Lace veil worn over your face.
Cathedral:	Falls three and a half yards from the headpiece. Ultra-formal.
Chapel:	Falls two and a half yards from the headpiece. Formal.
Fingertip:	It reaches to the fingertips, suitable for all gowns. Most popular style.
Flyaway:	Multiple layers that just brush your shoulders.

YOUR PERSONAL GUIDE TO FIGURE CAMOUFLAGE

As you shop for your perfect wedding gown, take along this guide to help you with style ideas.

THE BASICS

- Use detailing to draw attention where you want it and thus away from problem areas.

- The eye follows the lines of the gown.

- Vertical lines and seams add height and slenderize.

- Horizontal lines and seams shorten and widen the body.

- Diagonal and curved lines soften and add curves.

TOO THIN

- Draped styles and graceful flowing fabrics are ideal.
- Billowing sleeves conceal thin arms.
- Try a fitted waist, flowing skirt, and full sleeves.

TOO SHORT

- Draw eyes upward with detailing at your neck or bust.
- Have all lines and seams going vertically.
- Don't cut your body with waistlines or peplums.

THICK-WAISTED

- Straight gowns look the best.
- Don't emphasize the waist.
- Long line bras and bust to hip bustiers trim your waist.
- Strapless fitted gowns with stays mold a waistline.
- Diagonal beading slenderizes a waist.
- Try an empire or basque waist style or a strapless gown with an empire waist and flowing skirt.

HEAVY HIPS AND THIGHS

- Draw eyes up off lower body with bodice detailing, off the shoulder ruffles, puff sleeves, or fur trim across the shoulders.

- Flowing or flared skirts are best.

- Peplums and tulip overskirts can help conceal.

- Try an empire waist style with strapless or spaghetti straps in a flowing fabric.

SMALL-BUSTED

- Wear almost any style by padding the bustline.

- Draped, wrapped, or heavily beaded bodices add fullness.

- Wear a gown with sewn in bust cups.

- Conceal bust with a high neckline.

LARGE-BUSTED

- Wide skirt base and flared hems balance a large bust.

- V-neckline and sweetheart necklines are flattering.

- Try a beaded gown with a basque waistline.

NARROW SHOULDERS

- To broaden, draw the eye to the outer shoulders.

- Padded shoulders and puffed or gathered sleeves widen shoulders.

- Avoid halters or any top with lines aimed at the neck.

- Try a strapless gown with a long veil covering your shoulders.

- Your best bet is a widely scooped neckline or extra wide sweetheart neckline and padded shoulders.

SHORT-WAISTED

- Try a dropped waist, empire waist or hip-sashed gown.

- Straight gown lines can lengthen your torso.

- Avoid wide waistbands.

- Avoid wrap or diagonal bodices.

LONG-WAISTED

- No dropped waistlines or hip-sashed gowns.

- Try a wide waistband.

- An empire waist with flowing skirt conceals below the ribcage.

WIDE SHOULDERS

- Draw the eye inward toward the neck and face.
- Try halters, turtlenecks, or stand up beaded collars.
- Avoid padded shoulders.
- Try sheer lace sleeves, beaded bodice, and flowing skirt.
- Balance shoulders with a flared mermaid hem.
- Widen hips with a peplum or tulip skirt for balance.

SHORT NECK

- Try a V-neckline or sweetheart neckline.
- No high neck gowns or stand up collars.
- Try strapless or spaghetti strap gown styles.

THIN NECK

- Try high collars, beaded collars, or a soft ruffle.
- Avoid strapless gowns, revealing necklines, however, if it's a pretty neck, show it off!

YOUR PERFECT BRIDESMAID COLOR

Research has shown that colors have definite personalities. Use color psychology to help create the look of your wedding. Make sure the color you select flatters you, the bride, since you will be surrounded by it all day.

- White: Pure, clean, innocent, ladylike, classic
- Ivory: Elegant, refined, feminine, delicate
- Blue: Number-one favorite color, dignified, calm
- Navy: Traditional, reserved, official
- Aqua: Outgoing
- Yellow: Cheerful, friendly, outgoing
- Orange: Active, stimulating, enthusiastic, cheerful
- Green: Open, refreshing, restful, outdoorsy
- Dark Green: Refined
- Brown: Practical, reliable
- Gray/Silver: Classic, refined, elegant
- Purple: Dignified, royalty
- Wine/Burgundy: Regal, understated elegance, wealth
- Black: Sophisticated, dignified, elegant
- Pastels: Youthful, feminine, soothing, non-threatening
- Red: Exciting, confident, sexy, aggressive
- Pink: Feminine, delicate, spring

THE FINISHING TOUCHES

In much the same way that a quality frame finishes and compliments a masterpiece portrait, the final touches complete a bride's look to create a polished, finished look.

Proper undergarments are the foundation for that elegant look. Bridal undergarments include backless, long-line bras, bust-to-hip bustiers, bust cups, waist cinchers, and hosiery with built-in panties.

With the bust being an important feature in bridal gowns, the right brassiere is important. A good bra shapes, defines, supports, or even builds up the breasts. Many brides wear long-line bras or bust-to-hip bustiers, which provide support and create a sleek line, especially with the strapless gowns. To help simplify dressing, many designers sew brassiere cups or bustiers right into the gown.

It is important to note that since undergarments shape the body beneath the gown, they must be worn during fittings to ensure proper fit on your wedding day.

THE GARTER

Today's garter is a three- or four-inch-wide elastic band covered with satin or lace, often with an embroidered border decorated with bows, ribbons, pearls, or lace, and it is still thrown to the single men at your reception. A long-standing bridal superstition says that no harm can befall a bride wearing blue, so very often a bride selects a blue garter to throw and a white satin garter to keep.

THE BRIDE'S HANDBAG

A bride must decide what shape, size, fabric, and color handbag she should include with her ensemble, since her lipstick, pressed powder, perfume, and handkerchief must be kept on hand. While a shoulder strap design is rarely considered, any constructed, geometric shape such as a square, rectangle, or round is always in character. A traditional bag style is a soft white satin half-moon or pouch shape. The handbag that most brides bring along leans towards an unobtrusive evening size or clutch purse. The handbag's fabric can match, blend, or mix with the gown. The type of embellishment is coordinated with the dress in some way. For example, a handbag could be decorated with pearls, lace, rhinestones, sequins, jeweled buttons, beads, ribbons, and bows.

Sometimes an antique purse is selected to fill the tradition of something "old." Have your maid of honor carry your handbag for those quick touch ups before your portrait session.

What do I keep in my handbag?

- White tic-tac mints (Not green or red)
- Kleenex
- Lipstick
- Pressed powder compact
- Small spray perfume

Give your handbag to your maid of honor and when you need it, she'll have it. This is one less thing that you have to worry about.

DO I WEAR A COAT ON MY WEDDING DAY?

A bride needs a wrap or coat for only brief moments such as getting in and out of a car. Usually the gown's multi-layers of fabric are sufficient protection from the weather. However, in the evening, during the winter months or when inclement weather is expected, a loose-fitting matching or coordinated jacket, similar color cape, silk or satin wrap, shawl, or fur stole can be borrowed or rented and is carried by an attendant. It is unlikely that the guests will see you arrive; therefore, I wouldn't recommend spending a lot of money in this area of dressing.

JEWELRY

Jewelry enhances and finishes your bridal image. If your jewelry overpowers you and you see the jewelry before you see the bride, then it's inappropriate. You have to consider your dress design, facial shape, veil style, and hairstyle when selecting your jewelry.

THE POWER OF EARRINGS

Never underestimate the power of earrings. They are the jewels that dress your face. Earrings can accentuate the line of your neck or make your cheekbones stand out. They can draw attention to your hairstyle, your jaw line, and even your smile. Perhaps most importantly, earrings reflect the beauty of your eyes. Look at yourself in the mirror. First, you'll notice the sparkle and glow of your own eyes. Second, just beyond and slightly lower, you'll catch a second set of twinkling gems. When you think of it, earrings not only frame your face but also are really like another pair of beautiful eyes. Like our eyes, they speak volumes about who we are. Photographers often say that a person's eyes are the windows to their soul.

When purchasing your earrings, take into consideration your face shape, the hairstyle you will wear on your wedding day, and the neckline of your gown. If your features are small or your bone structure is delicate, you'll probably look best in petite button earrings, studs, or drops. If your features are strong or your bone structure is pronounced, larger, splashier earrings will probably flatter you best.

Your hairstyle is very important to consider. French twists and up-dos are a natural showcase for earrings and look great with everything from twinkling studs to shiny showstoppers. Longer, fuller hairstyles are more of a challenge. They call for earrings that stand out from the face yet don't get lost in the length of your hair or veil.

Besides choosing the right shaped earrings and the most flattering hairstyle, there are some great little tricks that can be played with earrings. A less than firm jaw line will tighten right up with the addition of large, strong clips, especially if they're geometrically shaped. Want to downplay a less favorite facial feature? Long, dangling earrings tend to slenderize the face because they accentuate length rather than width. Want to hide your earlobes? Button style earrings are a brilliant way to disguise that problem and many earrings combine both buttons and drops, helping to elongate your face.

When selecting your earrings, your options are almost unlimited. Consider where you will be seen in your earrings. For example, if you're having an evening reception, up-do hairstyles practically beg for big, dramatic earrings that glitter by candlelight. When you're going to be seen from a distance, go for drama. A small diamond stud will be hard to see for you guests in the back row.

Enjoy finding the perfect pair of earrings. Earrings, among their other powers, can make you feel feminine and elegant, and can really complete your total image.

THE ONE THING YOU SHOULD NEVER DO JUST BEFORE YOUR WEDDING STARTS

Picture this: It's only moments before you are to walk down the aisle. This is the moment you have dreamed of since you were a little girl. Your wedding gown has been meticulously chosen. Your veil is of timeless elegance. Your shoes are the perfect match, as though they were designed perfectly from the same bolt of fabric as your gown. Your nails are flawless. Your makeup is exquisite. Your hair has been carefully combed, teased, and coaxed into place. And to complete your reflection of beauty are your perfectly chosen earrings and necklace. Moments before you are to make your grand entrance you spray one last mist of hairspray to keep the illusion from melting, and you follow that up with a final spritz of perfume on your neck.

Believe it or not, those last minute sprays of hairspray and perfume are a *huge mistake*. That error was a simple one, repeated every day by women preparing for a day at the office, a beauty pageant, or their wedding day. You just coated your beautiful jewelry with thick, sticky hairspray! You have just dulled your pearls, diamonds, crystal, or rhinestones.

So, what is the best way to way to care for your jewelry? First, spray your hairspray and perfume before putting on your gown and headpiece. If you have to place your headpiece on first and work your hair around your veil, simply cover up any jewels that are on your veil and spray with the cover over your jewels. When spraying your perfume and hairspray, first remove your engagement ring. Therefore, when the photographer takes the classic portrait of your rings, your ring will sparkle in the photograph. (Please note to have your wedding ring set cleaned before your wedding day.)

Secondly, after you purchase your wedding jewelry, wrap each piece individually in a fleece material, such as sweatshirt. Do not let your pieces touch each other. Make sure your necklace is lying flat. While this might sound like a lot of work, it is really an investment that will allow you to enjoy your special jewelry for years to come.

Thirdly, clean your jewelry properly after wearing it. On diamonds, crystals, and rhinestones, simply use lukewarm water with very mild soap. Use a soft-bristled baby toothbrush to clean all the crevices. A soft brush won't loosen the setting and the mild soap won't harm the sealant and glues used in jewelry. Give it a good final rinse in cool to lukewarm water, and polish it with a soft flannel-type material. If you do this after every few wears, you won't have any spray build up. This is doubly important for necklaces worn on bare skin. Let your jewelry sparkle every day, just as you will on your wedding day!

MAKEUP TECHNIQUES THAT ENHANCE YOUR BEAUTY

The best beauty treatment for your skin is to fall in love and stay in love. Love gives an outer glow to your skin. You will have a brightness in your smile. Your eyes shine. The look of love photographs beautifully.

However, every bride can use makeup to enhance her looks. The key to successful makeup is learning how to bring your best features forward. This section provides tips on makeup understanding.

CONCEALER

Concealer is used to cover imperfections such as blemishes, scars, skin discolorations, and under-eye circles. Concealers are available in different consistencies ranging from creamy liquids to thick cake creams. Those with a thick consistency provide heavy coverage, which produces excellent results in photographs. A thin consistency will provide sheerness and minimal coverage. One of the most useful makeup products you should have for your wedding day is concealer in a pencil form. A concealer pencil can be used to retouch small areas that may need additional coverage after your makeup has been applied.

Your groom may benefit from using a concealer as well. He might need a little touch up on any facial blemishes. Because the color is sheer, the guests will not notice if he's wearing a very small bit of concealer. By using concealer to hide those blemishes, you will be very pleased with the great looking complexions you will see in your finished portraits!

Concealers are made in a wide range of flesh tones, as well as white, which dramatically lightens areas. Lavender concealers help mask yellow areas; green concealers combat red tones in your skin. Select a concealer that is nearly opaque and half a shade lighter than your complexion.

FOUNDATION

Foundation is used to create attractive skin tones by evening out the texture and color of your complexion, concealing imperfections, setting a base for the rest of your makeup, and protecting your skin.

Foundations are available in different forms and

consistencies. They range from thin, watery liquids to creams, foams, powders, gels, sticks, cakes, and pancakes. The opacity, or covering ability, of a foundation is also important to consider. The different degrees of coverage range from heavy to medium to sheer. Finish is another distinguishing characteristic. A matte foundation gives a soft, powdery, non-shine finish. This is the best look for photographs. A glossy foundation gives a dewy or shiny look. The camera picks up on any bit of shine, which will make your face appear greasy. Semi-matte foundations appear neither shiny nor powdery. Again, this results in a very good look in photographs. The contents of a foundation also have an effect on the skin and the appearance created. Most foundations have either an oil or water base. Oil-based foundations tend to be richer and more beneficial to dry skin. Water-based foundations create a very sheer look and work well on oily skin.

Because foundations are available in a wide range of flesh tones, selecting the perfect shade is critical. Always check colors in natural light. Using a sponge, apply the foundation to your cheek above the jaw. The color should match the skin on your neck. Usually beige-toned foundations look most attractive in portraits. Those with reddish or orange tones often look unnatural, especially for portraits taken outdoors. If your skin has golden or warm undertones, select a beige foundation with a hint of peach, gold, yellow, or tawny color. If your skin has blue, pink, or cool undertones, select an ivory foundation or one with a hint of pinkish color. It's important that you don't deviate too far from your skin's natural coloring.

Once you have applied foundation to your face, there should never be a noticeable difference between the color of your face and your neck. Always blend foundation well into your hairline and under your jawbone. There should never be a line of demarcation. Finish your foundation application by using downward strokes to make your facial hair lie down.

POWDER

Powder is used to smooth and refine your skin, add coverage to your foundation, and create a base for application of powdered makeup such as blush and eyeshadow. It also gives your face a matte finish, which is crucial for attractive photographs. Powder is most useful for diminishing unattractive shine caused by oil and perspiration, especially on your nose, forehead, and chin. Applying powder is an important final step, as it sets your makeup so that it won't move, fade, or change color.

Powder is available in two basic forms: loose or compressed. Loose powder is applied with a large powder puff and will give you a smooth, evenly-finished look. Compressed or pressed powders are packaged in compacts and are convenient for touch-ups all throughout your wedding day.

Powder is available in light, medium, and dark

flesh tones as well as in white, pink, peach, and lavender. Metallic flecked powders are not recommended for photographs. Powder is available in three degrees of opacity: opaque, translucent, and transparent.

For your wedding day portraits, select a matte, translucent face powder that matches your foundation. Use peach, pink, or mauve to enliven a dull, grayish skin tone. Select lavender to tone down sallow skin.

SPECIAL TECHNIQUES ON CONTOURING AND HIGHLIGHTS

Contouring and highlighting techniques are used to correct, improve, change, or enhance the structure and features of the face. Contour makeup is darker and duller than the complexion. Dark or dull colors make the area on which they are applied appear to recede. Highlight makeup emphasizes, enlarges, and brings forward areas on which it has been applied. Highlight makeup is lighter, brighter, or shinier than the complexion.

Both contour and highlight makeup are available in cream or powder form Contour makeup is available in a wide range of dark flesh tones. Cool-toned matte makeup tends to contour best. Highlight makeup is available in a wide range of light flesh tones as well as white, light yellow, light pink, and pearlized gold or silver.

For very subtle contouring, use foundation or face powder in a shade darker than your complexion. For very subtle highlighting, select foundation or powder a shade lighter than your complexion.

HINTS ON CONTOURING AND HIGHLIGHTING

- Your contouring and highlighting should never be obvious. Always use it *sparingly* and blend well.

- Use a sponge to apply your contour or highlight cream to your cheeks, jawbone, and forehead. Use a contour brush to apply contour powder in these same areas. Use a fan brush to apply highlight powders.

- To contour your nose with contour cream, use a sponge-tipped applicator or your index finger. To contour your nose with contour powder, use an eyeshadow fluff brush.

- To highlight the bridge of your nose, your lips, or other small areas, use the pad of your index finger to apply creams or a sponge-tipped applicator with either powders or creams.

- Always finish your contour/highlight application with translucent loose powder.

- The figures that follow show the effects created when contour or highlight makeup is used in the designated areas.

Forehead

Contour: Shortens a high forehead. Evens an uneven hairline when contour matches hair color.

Highlight: Lengthens a short forehead.

Contour: Rounds a square forehead.

Highlight: Gives width to a round forehead.

Contour: Flattens a protruding forehead.

Highlight: Brings forward an indented forehead. Enlarges forehead.

Contour: Narrows a wide forehead. Elongates a short forehead.

Highlight: Widens a narrow forehead.

Contour: Narrows a wide forehead.

Highlight: Lengthens a short forehead.

Temples

Contour: Narrows wide set eyes. Adds shape to face. Gives and uplifting look to eyes. Slims a wide or round face.

Highlight: Widens narrow set eyes. Increases width of face at eye line.

Eyes

Contour: Diminishes a puffy underbrow.

Highlight: Lifts arch of eyebrow. Give a dramatic look to brows.

AMIE WITKOWSKI

Contour: Reshapes brow. Brings brow closer to eye. Defines bridge of nose.

Highlight: Lifts brow, opens eye. Makes eyes seem wider set.

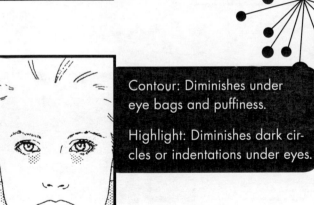

Contour: Diminishes under eye bags and puffiness.

Highlight: Diminishes dark circles or indentations under eyes.

Eyes

Contour: Adds shape to outer eye area and temples. Uplifts eyes and face.

Highlight: Expands the temples area. Opens up the face, yielding a brighter look.

Contour: Diminishes prominent eyelids.

Highlight: Draws attention to irises. Brings deep-set eyes forward. Enlarges upper lid.

Face

Contour: Not used in this area.

Highlight: Brings cheekbones up and forward. Emphasizes eyes. Diminishes shadows under eyes.

Contour: Heightens cheekbones. Slims a full face or cheeks.

Highlight: Fills out a thin face.

Face

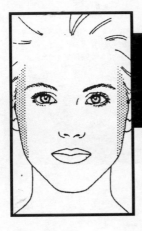

Contour: Slims a wide face.

Highlight: Widens a narrow face.

Contour: Pushes back fleshy areas around nose but may make nose seem more prominent.

Highlight: Gives a healthy, youthful, rounded appearance to cheeks. Highlights apples of cheeks.

Nose

Contour: Pushes back
a protruding nose.

Highlight: Brings a flat nose
forward. Slims a wide nose.
Elongates a short nose.

Contour: Shortens a long nose.

Highlight: Gives the illusion of a turned-up nose.

Nose

Contour: Diminishes fullness around nose and mouth.

Highlight: Brings out depressions around nose and in laugh lines.

Contour: Shortens a long nose. Diminishes tip on a turned-down nose.

Highlight: Lengthens nose. Turns up tip of nose when blended upward.

Nose

Contour: Narrows or defines sides of nose. Elongates nose. Diminishes bumps on nose when contour is applied to protrusions.

Highlight: Widens a narrow nose. Shortens a long nose. Diminishes bumps on nose when highlighter is applied to indentations.

Contour: Gives shape to a flat nose. Raises or lowers a low or high nose bridge. Shortens a long nose.

Highlight: Widens a small or narrow nose bridge. Brings forward a deep indentation at nose bridge. Raises a low nose bridge.

Nose

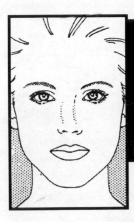

Contour: Eliminates a crooked nose. Contour side of nose that curves outward.

Highlight: Eliminates a crooked nose. Highlight side of nose that indents.

Contour: Narrows a wide nose bridge. Defines inner eye area at bridge of nose. Balances width of bridge with end of nose.

Highlight: Widens a narrow nose bridge. Makes narrow set eyes seem wide set.

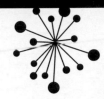

Jaw and Chin

Contour: Balances a lopsided jaw or asymmetrical face or lips. Apply contour to excessive side.

Highlight: Balances a lopsided jaw or asymmetrical face or lips. Apply highlight to deficient side.

Contour: Diminishes a large chin.

Highlight: Lengthens a short chin.

Jaw and Chin

Contour: Pushes back a protruding chin.

Highlight: Diminishes a cleft chin when applied just in indentation.

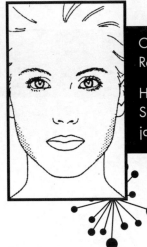

Contour: Slims a wide jaw. Rounds a square jaw.

Highlight: Widens jaw. Squares a round or sloping jaw. Emphasizes cheek hollows.

Jaw and Chin

Contour: Defines jaw, separating face from neck. Shade along jawline from earlobe to earlobe.

Highlight: Softens an angular or bony jaw.

Contour: Diminishes a fleshy or double chin.

Highlight: Is not used in this area.

Jaw and Chin

Contour: Creates a slight indentation under lip to give chin more shape and shorten.

Highlight: Brings out a deep indentation under lower lip.

Contour: Rounds a pointed chin. Shortens a long chin.

Highlight: Brings forward a receding chin.

BLUSH

Blush is available in liquid, cream, cake, gel, powder-cream, and powder forms. Blush is available in a variety of shades of red, pink, orange or coral, purple or plum, brown and gold. They are also available in different finishes such as matte, frosted, glossy, and lightly pearlized. Blush gives a healthy glow and accents your cheeks.

If your skin is oily, use powder blush. If your skin is dry, use cream blush for a very natural look. Gels are best for flawless, young skin and are most effective when used on bare skin. Liquids are best used as all-over color washes or for just a hint of color. If your skin exhibits yellow or warm tones, select peach, golden, beige, coral, or tawny colors. If your skin is pinkish or has cool tones, select colors with a hint of pink such as rose, plum, or fuchsia. Always apply blush sparingly and blend well. To ensure that your blush color is subtly blended, stroke lightly over the edges of your application with a clean foam sponge.

LIP COLOR

Lip makeup can define, correct, or alter the natural shape of your lips. Color your lips to draw attention to and accent them. Lip makeup is available in four basic forms: lip pencils to outline your lips, lipsticks and lip creams to color your lips, and lip glosses or tints to add shine or a touch of color to your lips. Lip primers are also made to condition the lips and to set a base for long-lasting lip color.

Select a colorless lip primer rich in emollients, such as Chapstick, and use it daily to prevent dryness and chapping. Select cool color lipsticks or lip creams to make your teeth appear brighter and whiter. Cool colors include reds, cool reds, blue-pinks, plums, icy-pinks, and violets. Be careful if you select warm tone lipsticks or lip creams, as they can bring out the yellow in your teeth, making your teeth appear dull. Warm colors include orange, coral, and apricot. Select lip-lining pencils to match your lip color. On your wedding day, use a matte or semi-frost lip color. Stay away from heavy frosts, especially pinks, as frosts tend to make your smile look faded. You can use a gloss on your special day, but go easy on it. Remember, you will be kissing a lot of people and your gloss will tend to smear outside your lip line. (For your engagement portrait or bridal portrait, wear a gloss because the camera favors glossy lips in studio conditions.)

EYE MAKEUP

Eye makeup is used to enlarge your eyes as well as improve, define, or exaggerate their shape and to enhance the color of your eyes.

Eyeshadows in pressed powder form are most effective in portraits. Select neutral, unfrosted colors such as beige, brown, gray, navy, and soft pinks. These colors will help accentuate your eyes yet have them still appear natural. When using your eyeliner, rest the heel of your hand or your little finger on your cheek to anchor and steady your hand during application. Line as close to your lash line as possible. Always smudge your eyeliner on your lower lash line for a softer, more natural look. Smudge your liner with a cotton swab or a sponge-tipped applicator.

Always complete your eye makeup with waterproof mascara. Position your wand at the base of your lashes, and move it slowly outward toward the tips of your lashes using a slight side-to-side motion. Use the tip of the mascara wand to coat lashes at the outer corners of your eyes, which can easily be missed.

The following examples provide suggestions on how to use makeup to accentuate your eyes, regardless of their size and shape.

SMALL SET EYES

Small eyes will look larger if they seem to be set in a pool of color. Generally, shadow darker than the eye color will be better than pale or frosted shadows. Leave a space between the eye color and the eyebrows. When using eyeliner, draw a thin line that lifts to a pcak just above the pupil. Use a soft, off black or brown eyeliner. Draw a very thin line, in a lighter shade, under the lower lash line. Draw the line slightly beyond the iris, but not extending beyond the corners of the eye.

PROTRUDING EYES

Protruding eyes can be minimized by applying flat medium tones shadowed over the entire upper eyelids up to the brow area. Avoid using frosted, shiny colors. Apply a darker flat shadow over three quarters of the eyelid from lash to crease. Eyeliner applied from corner to corner on the upper lid will further minimize the problem.

DROOPY OUTER CORNERS

Droopy eyes can be made to look more lifted by blending shadow or color upward and outward toward the lip of the brow. Eyeliner should not follow the downward curve of the lid. Curl lashes and apply mascara to the outer lashes.

ROUND EYES

Round eyes need to be downplayed to minimize their round appearance. Apply a deeper shadow over the prominent part of the eyelids, blending it outward toward the brow. Apply a soft line at the outer part of the lower lid. Use mascara only on the outer part of the upper lashes.

DEEP-SET EYES

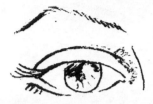 

Deep-set eyes need to be brought forward by using light matte colors. Smudge soft colors from the lashes right up to the brow to open up and bring eyes forward. Lighten the under eye area. Line only the upper lash line in a medium tone, lifting the line at the end. The eyeliner can be fairly wide.

HIDDEN LIDS

Hidden lids need more interest. Create a crease in the middle of the upper lid and highlight the brow bone. Upper and lower lashes can be lined softly with color. Small, false eyelashes help the illusion. Avoid very strong colors.

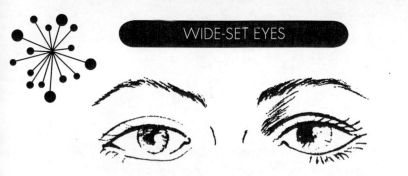

WIDE-SET EYES

Wide-set eyes will seem closer together when shadow is applied on the eyelid, inward toward the tear ducts. Avoid winging color upward and outward. Eyes will appear closer together if the inner corner of the brows are brought in line with the tear duct. The eyeliner can be fairly wide.

CLOSE-SET EYES

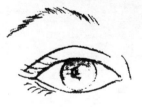 

Close-set eyes will seem farther apart when the brows are tweezed a bit wider apart and the inner corner of the eye lightened with foundation. Shade the outer half of the lid with a dark color and extend the color toward the temples. A line that starts thinly over the iris and thickens as it extends beyond the outer corner gives the illusion of more width between the eyes.

SELF-TANNING LOTIONS

Self-tanning products contain the chemical dihydroxy-acetone (DHA), an ingredient that has long been FDA approved as a food colorant. When applied to the skin, it reacts with the proteins and amino acids in the skin's surface layer and produces a brown skin tone. Today's self-tanning lotions have improved significantly in their color and odor compared to the products of several years ago. Test the product first on the inside of your arm to be sure you like the results.

Even application is critical to achieving an even tan. Since most formulas disappear into the skin right away, it's sometimes hard to know exactly how much you've applied until the color develops. Dry skin tends to absorb more formula, leading to streaks. For best results, exfoliate and shower to smooth and hydrate your skin before applying a tanning product.

When applying self-tanning lotion to your face, work in small sections, massaging the self-tanner into the skin to cover evenly. Don't leave a chin line. Cover your neck too. If your gown is low-cut or off the shoulder, make sure you cover all exposed areas.

Your tan should last three to five days, until the surface of your skin has naturally shed.

Experiment with sunless tanning lotion several

weeks prior to your wedding so that you will be familiar with the look you want to achieve.

YOUR CAPTIVATING FRAGRANCE

Perfume has a magic way of enhancing your personality and adding the final touch to your wedding attire. A spray of the right scent can make you feel romantic, feminine, and sensuous. Fragrance can evoke mystery and add drama. It can make you feel luxurious and elegant. Fragrance creates an impression that becomes part of your total beauty. Choose your fragrance with the same careful thought you have put into selecting your wedding gown.

Fragrances fall into six general categories according to their composition and aroma. While each type is distinctive and specific, the categories may overlap.

THE SIX FRAGRANCE TYPES

- **Single Flower Fragrance:** This is the scent of one flower only, such as a rose or a gardenia. This scent is charming and appropriate in the spring and summer months. This fragrance is best suited for the feminine personality.

- **Floral Bouquet Fragrance:** The floral bouquet scent, in general, has a wearability that's hard to beat. This fragrance is like pearls—it never fails!

This scent is usually a blend of flowers such as roses, carnations, and lily of the valley. This fragrance expresses the romantic personality.

- **Woodsy Fragrance:** This fresh outdoor fragrance is perfect for outdoor weddings. The scent is reminiscent of herbs, leaves, ferns, and woods. This fragrance is naturally fresh and alive. It is wonderful for the outdoor, all-around good sport type.

- **Fruit Fragrance:** This exhilarating fragrance seems to burst with glorious scent. It offers a sunny warmth when mixed with florals such as roses and jasmine. This fragrance is classically French. It is ideal for the refined, traditional bride. She's distinguished and has an aura of graciousness.

- **Oriental Fragrance:** This scent is wonderful for after-five wear on the sophisticated and sometimes daring woman. It is the strongest and longest lasting of all fragrances. This sultry and exotic fragrance is made up of spices, vanilla, incense, and other aromatic ingredients. This fragrance is bold and warmly mysterious.

- **Spice Fragrance:** This fragrance is sophisticated, rich, and elegant. The spice fragrance is a blend of pine, citrus, forest, and mossy notes. It is a sharp and clean-cut scent. It is a favorite of several personality types, since it is youthful, alive, and very contemporary. It is great for day-time wear.

FIVE WAYS TO CREATIVELY USE YOUR FRAGRANCE

- For your bridal shower, register for your favorite fragrance. This way you can have it for your wedding day. Remember to include bubble bath, shower gel, powder, and lotion all in your special scent. Layering fragrances with several products will give it better wearability throughout the day.

- Spray your silk flower arrangements and your silk bouquets with your perfume.

- Spray your pew bows one hour before your wedding begins. As your guests are walking down the aisle, they will smell your delightful fragrance.

- Use plug-in air fresheners at the church or reception. Plug them in the night before the wedding so it has a chance to release its full scent that compliments your fresh flowers.

- Make a sachet by saturating a cotton ball with your perfume and place it in your bra. Your body temperature will release the scent throughout the day.

- Make fragrance a part of your personal beauty statement. Perfume is the finishing touch to a perfectly groomed and totally beautiful you.

YOUR PERFECT HANDS

"To have and to hold, from this day forth ..."

Of course, you want your groom to hold the perfect hands on your perfect day. Think of your nails as jewels, decorative accents for your hands. Your nails can have a romantic drawing power when they are shaped as colorful ovals, glowing like gems. Use nail polish to accent your color scheme as well as to make your hands more beautiful.

EIGHT STEPS TO A PROFESSIONAL MANICURE

Exfoliate

Use a facemask to treat your hands and feet. A mud mask works wonderfully.

File

An emery board is easier on the nail than a metal file. The thinner your nail, the finer the emery board should be. File in one direction only, preferably from the side toward the center. Avoid filing down too far. Shape

your nail to your liking. Some brides like the look of oval nails, while others prefer square nails. Either shape photographs beautifully.

Soak

Soak your fingers in warm, soapy water. If your fingers are discolored, take a tablet of denture cleanser and dissolve it in the water.

Care for Your Cuticles

Apply cuticle softener to the edge of your nails or let your hand soak in warm olive oil for a few minutes. This will really soften your cuticles and make your hands feel wonderful. Using a cuticle pusher or cutter, push back the cuticle and cut away any excess hangnails. Don't cut in to your cuticle because it will cause it to bleed. Do not get in the habit of cutting your cuticles, as it will only make them tougher. Only cut your hangnails.

Massage

Apply a moisturizer all over your hands, rubbing it into your nails and cuticles.

Wipe

Dip a cotton ball in an astringent and remove any excess oil off your fingernails. This is necessary to allow polish to go on smoothly without bubbling.

Apply the Base Coat

Apply a base coat or primer and allow it to dry thoroughly.

Apply the Top Final Coat

Brush on one-coat polish. Look for the kind that contains both a color and topcoat. It's just as good as using two separate products, and it's a great time saver.

ARTIFICIAL NAILS

There's nothing more flattering to your hands than exquisite nails that make your fingers look longer, your hands slimmer and more elegant. Brides who constantly have their hands on display rely on artificial nails to complete their well-groomed look and to provide that extra touch of glamour. If you are not used to artificial nails, have them put on at least four weeks prior to your wedding. This will give you ample time to get used to them.

BEAUTY TIPS FOR HANDS AND NAILS

- Color: Dark polish makes your nails look smaller; medium polish makes your nails look larger; and light polish makes your nails look delicate. Exaggerated dark or trendy colors are not recommended for photographs.

- If you are having your nails polished for the wedding, coordinate the color with your bridal bouquet. For example, a bouquet of red roses would call for red nail polish. A bouquet of stargazer lilies would call for a shade of pink, while a bouquet of white flowers surrounded by greenery would call for a French manicure. Incidentally, a French manicure is a beautiful compliment to any type of bouquet because of its classic, timeless look.

- Always coordinate your polish to your lip color.

- Make sure to pack some sixty-second-drying nail polish for your honeymoon. This is one time you will not want to be waiting for your polish to dry.

Use these four tips for the perfect portrait of your hand in his, highlighting your wedding rings.

Give your groom a manicure. Not only will his hands look great for your ring portrait, but it will make him feel special, too.

Cover any scrapes or scratches on your hands with concealer before the portrait is taken. This can save you money on having the photograph retouched.

Clean your rings the day *before* your wedding, not the day of your wedding. Nerves will be high on the wedding day, and you do not want to risk accidentally dropping the ring down the drain with unsteady hands.

Before your ring portrait is taken, apply hand lotion. This will make your hands appear soft and supple.

YOUR ENGAGEMENT RING

After all of your efforts to ensure your hands and nails look their best, do not let their beauty be undermined by a dingy engagement ring. Dip your engagement ring in jewelry cleaner to give it the sparkle it deserves next to your beautiful nails.

Supplies

- Shower gel for soaking
- Polish remover
- Polish
- Nail file
- Foot file
- Heavy socks
- Vaseline
- Tissue or a sponge toe separator

Steps

- Soak your feet to soften the skin. Use your foot file to smooth out heel calluses.
- Separate toes with a tissue or sponge toe separator.
- Apply polish remover to eliminate oils from the skin.
- File nails to a square shape. Run the file horizontally over the nail to prevent future snags.
- Apply a base coat. Your nail polish will look much richer with a base coat.
- Apply polish.
- Brush nails with oil to prevent ridges from forming.
- Sit back, put your feet up, and dream about your big day while your polish dries!

** To really soften the heels of your feet, apply a thick coat of Vaseline all over your feet, put on thick cotton socks. It's best to do this before bed, as the Vaseline will soften your skin while you sleep, and by morning, you will have soft and smooth heels and feet.

PERFECT POSTURE

It is worthwhile to learn a graceful walk, just as it is worthwhile to learn the importance of great posture. Your posture tells the world how to treat you. Posture tells others what to think of you from sight alone. Poor posture can make you look tired, bored, and pained—anything but sleek and sexy. Poor posture will certainly diminish the poise, elegance, and confidence you want to project.

Did you know, for instance, that you can add as much as two inches to your height just by stretching up through your spine? That's right! That's why dancers are so enviably tall and graceful. They understand the importance of proper alignment and posture.

In addition to the aesthetic benefits of good posture, it has therapeutic benefit as well. With muscles holding our bones in good position, there's room for the healthy functioning of the internal organs. As a result, our nerves don't get pinched and those wearisome aches and pains will usually go away.

Sounds simple? It is! Your upper torso is your key to good posture. Pull your entire ribcage up as high as you can while standing, walking, and sitting. Widen the space between your navel and your ribs. Feel the space widen from your navel as you pull your ribcage up. Another way to practice great posture is to pretend you have a helium-filled balloon tied with a piece of string to the top of your head. The balloon is constantly raising your posture up, all the while keeping your head held high and keeping your head level.

Good posture improves health, increases stamina, and enhances body control. In addition, it is amazing to see what good posture does for the way you appear in your gown. Your gown has been designed to hang beautifully on a bride with good posture, not over the humps and bulges caused by poor posture. So, to reflect your look of poise and self-esteem, make good posture a part of your everyday routine and on your wedding day it will be very natural.

YOUR GRACEFUL WALK

On this very special day you will want to be enchanting and captivating, not only to your groom, but also to your guests. To achieve this special grace you will need to begin practicing your walk. A bride who walks beautifully is a delight to behold. Of all the qualities you can develop, this is one quality that will make you admired, even after your wedding day. Your walk tells a great deal about you. It can bespeak your loveliness.

A beautiful walk should appear effortless and smooth. Use these three steps to make the most of your gait.

1. Begin practicing walking with your wedding shoes on. The shoe you select must feel comfortable in order for you to look fluid and poised. *Do not begin breaking in your shoes the morning of your wedding!* Begin breaking in your shoes at least three weeks prior to the wedding. When your day comes, your shoes will fit like gloves and will allow you to dance the evening through. Your wedding day is not the day to wear three-and-a-half inch heels if you are not used to wearing them. Stick to the heel height you feel most comfortable in.

2. Poise and balance are synonymous. If a beautiful walk is anything, it is well balanced. You must not "settle" with each step. You must think tall and light. There should not be any perceptive change of weight from one foot to the other. This can be achieved by keeping the weight on the balls of your feet and by "pushing off" with the back of your foot. If you sink onto your heels, your walk will lack the stately quality that a bride should possess. Your knees should remain flexed so that they act as the "spring" for the body, giving your walk a smooth, fluid appearance.

3. One foot should be placed directly in front of the other on one line. The direction of your walk must be forward, not up and down or from side to side. Try to acquire and evenly spaced momentum. This

method gives a feminine look and when done with balance and grace is called a "model's walk."

YOUR GRAND ENTRANCE

When making your *grand entrance* down the aisle, *pause* at the doorway. This one small gesture will allow you to take everything in and also allows your guests to see you in full view.* This is your moment! This will be the moment you capture your groom's heart forever! Remember to keep your bouquet at your waist. (When nervous, most brides hold their bouquets too high, hiding all the detail of their bodice.) Now begin your journey down the aisle with your timeless grace and effortless walk.

When making your grand entrance at the reception, remember again to *pause* at the door. After hearing "And now may I present to you the new Mr. and Mrs…" Do not rush in! Smile, take a deep breath, and pause. You will never be able to take this moment back. Walk in with your head held high knowing this is going to be the greatest night of your life!

This will also give your photographer the opportunity to take a full-length portrait of you.

A TREASURE CHEST
of Image Ideas

- Experiencing puffy eyes? Lie down with cold spoons, cucumber slices, or wet tea bags over your eyes. Any of these three items should reduce your puffiness.

- One week before the wedding, do not use any new products, such as laundry detergent or fabric softeners. Your skin may break out from them. Also note, if you dry your hair with towels that have been dried with fabric sheets, this may cause your hair to go limp. The softener from the towels will coat your freshly-washed wet hair.

- Make sure you eat on the morning of your wedding! Many times brides skip breakfast. This is a bad mistake, since you won't have time to eat until much later in the day. By not eating breakfast, you will lack energy, and you certainly need all the

energy you can muster on your wedding day! In both your groom's and your dressing rooms, provide a snack tray for you and the wedding party. Make sure the tray includes non-staining items such as cheese, crackers, fruit, etc.

- Bridesmaids should wear a clear deodorant/anti-perspirant—not a white solid—if their dresses are dark and sleeveless.

- One month before your big day, begin drinking eight glasses of water a day. This will ensure a glowing complexion, which the camera loves. (If you are not used to drinking this level of water, don't fret. Your initial frequent trips to the restroom will subside as your body learns to accommodate the increased volume of fluids!)

- Having a beautiful smile no longer has to cost a fortune. Check with your dentist for information on all the affordable new ways to improve your teeth.

- About three months prior to your wedding, begin using a whitening toothpaste. Whiter teeth will enhance your smile. The camera favors a bright smile.

- For an instant lift, highlight your hair. It will bring light to your face. The camera always favors highlights.

- If you aren't happy with the texture of your hair, simply switch shampoos. Sometimes a slight difference in ingredients will change the way your hair looks and behaves.

- One of the most important reasons to get your body in shape is not to lose weight, but for the graceful movement and better carriage. Proper carriage is one of the best ways to camouflage extra pounds!

- Try not to lose any weight after your final dress fitting. You will want your bodice to lie flat and fit perfectly.

- Consider your heel height, your headpiece, and the "up-do" of your hairstyle. All can add a good two inches to your height possibly making you taller than your groom.

- Your posture should be graceful and elegant. Carriage and posture affects how your gown looks. You need to stand with your shoulders back and your abdomen up and in. Practice! Practice! Practice!

- Pre-record a poem for your groom, or a special message from both of you to your parents. Play it on the church's sound system just before you walk down the aisle.

- Get plenty of rest the week of your wedding.

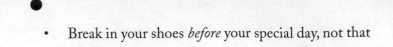

- Break in your shoes *before* your special day, not that day!

- Begin working with your hair stylist about a month before your wedding to determine just the "right look" for you with your headpiece.

- Wear solid colors for your engagement portrait. A print is too distracting to the eye. Coordinate your colors to match your fiancée.

- Make sure you highlight *underneath* your hair, especially if you plan to wear your hair pulled up. Often the top of your hair is blonde but underneath is dark, causing a big contrast in your portraits.

- Eyebrows! Pluck them, shape them, define them, but don't forget them! Your eyebrows frame your face.

- Consider the fabric of the mothers and grandmothers gown. Often their dresses are sheer and cannot support a pinned-on heavy corsage. A better choice might be a wrist corsage or a nosegay (a small hand held bouquet.)

- At the church rehearsal, pre-light your altar candles. In the shipping process, chances are the wicks have been pressed down into the wax. By pre-lighting your candles, it will ensure your ushers will be

able to light the candles effortlessly on your wedding day.

- A maid of honor is single. A matron of honor is married.

- Your garter is worn on your left leg, closest to your heart.

- Pick up the wedding gown and tuxedo the day before your wedding. The less you have to do the morning of your wedding, the calmer you will be.

- Consider adding fur trim to your winter wedding dress. Your attendants and flower girl could also carry decorated fur muffs instead of bouquets.

- Pay close attention to the back of your gown. During many ceremonies, this is the view the congregation has for the longest amount of time.

- If you want to counter bad breath, small mints such as tic tacs are an excellent choice. Stay away from large breath mints, as they are bulky and will be noticeable to your guests. *Never, never* chew gum. It is very distracting. Make sure your wedding party avoids gum as well. Chewing gum tends to take away the elegance of your whole attire.

- Never wear a watch with your wedding gown.

- Stay away from iridescent eyeshadows if you want to de-emphasize wrinkles and sagging lids.

- Take a full-length mirror to the church if your dressing room doesn't provide one.

- Make sure both you and each bridesmaid brings a spare pair of nylons.

- Remind your groom to shave *very carefully*. He will be nervous too, and any nicks or small cuts caused by his razor will show up in every photograph. Should this happen, he may need to use a little concealer to cover the nick or cut.

- Remind flower girls to always lift up their dresses before walking up a staircase.

- If you're unsure whether your flower girl or ring bearer will walk down the aisle, have a small toy waiting at the end of the aisle for them. Sometimes the special "prize" will help coax them down.

- If you would like your flower girl or ring bearer to stand up at the altar with your adult attendants, have a small white wicker chair, possibly decorated with tulle, in case they get tired of standing through the service. This way they won't be a distraction.

- A young person can be your Bible bearer. They would bring the Bible to the altar for the minister to read from. This Bible becomes the bride and groom's family heirloom to pass onto their children one day.

- If you have a very young flower girl or ring bearer, spray paint a wagon white and decorate it with silk ivy and soft tulle/netting and have an older child attendant pull them down the aisle.

- Young children can be bell-ringers. They walk in just before the bride's entrance, and "herald" the bride in.

- If you would like to have young attendants in your wedding, first consider their ages. Although children mature at different levels, some recommended guidelines are:

  - Flower girls and ring bearers: 4–8 years of age
  - Junior bridesmaids and ushers: 9–14 years of age

- At your rehearsal dinner, give out a time schedule to everyone involved with the wedding. This will tell everyone who needs to be where and at what time. It is extremely important to keep everyone well informed.

- If your dressing room isn't carpeted, bring along a bed sheet to stand on after you have put on your

gown. After all, you don't want your beautiful dress to be dusting the floor.

- Have your aisle runner already in place and tacked down with tape or pins. Have this done before your guests arrive. If you don't have a flower girl, scatter rose petals down the aisle prior to the guests arriving. For fall weddings, scatter various colored silk leaves down the aisle in copper, gold, brown, and burgundy colors.

- Have your groom carry tissues with him during the ceremony. In case either of you tear up you will be ready. You may also wrap your bouquet with tissue.

- Practice perfect posture.

- Kleenex boxes should be in the parents' pews before the wedding begins. Mothers shouldn't carry a purse down the aisle.

- Do not fill your flower girls basket to the rim with flower petals. She will drop many of them before she even makes it to the aisle. (Most flower girls are very bouncy moments before the ceremony begins.)

- Makeup tip for flower girls and junior bridesmaids:
  - Eyeshadow—Soft peach, dusty pinks
  - Blush—A whisper pink

- Lipstick—A light pink, not a heavy lip-gloss

- Nails—Lavender, pinks, peaches

- Just don't over do it with your little ones. Have them look their age

- Your bouquet should rest on your hipbones. Many times the bride and her bridesmaids carry their bouquet to high and hide all the detailing on their bodice.

- If you want a more intimate feel on your altar, fill the space with over-sized ferns and blooming plants. Take them into the reception and give them away at the end of the night to the special people who have helped you that day (cake attendants, guest book helpers, personal attendant, host and hostess, master of ceremonies, etc.)

- Have attendants face out toward the congregation. The congregation will enjoy watching their faces and they, in turn, will enjoy being able to see yours.

- During the wedding ceremony, have your maid/ matron of honor fluff out your train. A full train photographs much better from the back when it is straightened out rather than wrinkled from just having walked down the aisle. Plus, it's more visually appealing to the guests.

- Don't start lighting the unity candle until the music

begins. Often brides and grooms are done lighting their candle at the beginning of the music.

- In place of throwing the bouquet and garter, give the bouquet and garter to the longest-married couple at your wedding reception.

- A quick paced solution to the traditional receiving line is to usher the guests out yourselves. Your parents may receive your guests at the back of the church.

- If you and you groom usher your guests out of the sanctuary, do not hold your bouquet. With all the hugging and kissing you will be doing, your bouquet will only get in the way and will wilt really fast.

- Re-apply your lipstick and powder after dinner. You'll want to look fresh for the cake cutting ceremony.

- Display your grandparents' and parents' wedding portraits at the reception.

- Change into a pair of flats at the reception if you plan to dance a lot. Changing your heel height can revitalize you. But please, don't go barefoot. A bare foot ruins your elegant image.

- For an evening reception, rhinestone earrings can make your eyes sparkle, especially by candlelight.

- Buy yourself a basket of goodies to take with you on your honeymoon:

  - A facial mask—a refreshing way to energize your skin.

  - Foot lotion for your dancing feet

  - Deep conditioner for your hair. Your hair needs a little extra attention after enduring the weight of your headpiece and all the products you used on your hair.

  - Bubble bath and candles for some much needed quiet time with your groom

• THESE ARE THE THREE THINGS THAT OFTEN GET LEFT BEHIND AT HOME

1. The bride's garter. Make sure you pack your garter with your bridal gown.

2. The cake knife. Possibly give your cake knife to the florists if they will be decorating your cake with fresh flowers.

3. The wedding programs. Bring your programs the night of your rehearsal and make sure you tell the ushers where you have put them. Often they get hidden out of sight and are never handed out.

- *Finally,* relax and enjoy every minute of your special day, a day you have dreamed of and planned for a very long time. Today, your timeless beauty and grace will remain in your groom's heart forever.

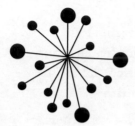

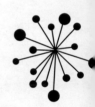

HOW TO BE A BEAUTIFUL BRIDE

AMIE WITKOWSKI
MEISTER-WITKOWSKI PHOTOGRAPHY

5684 ST. JOSEPH AVENUE
STEVENSVILLE, MICHIGAN 49127
(269) 429-9988

Photo Album